Classic Cocktail Guides
and Retro Bartender Books

Nineteenth-Century Cocktail Creations

How to Mix Drinks: A Bar Keeper's Handbook

George Winter

Historic Cookbooks of the World
Kalevala Books, Chicago

"Wine is sunlight, held together by water."
— Galileo Galilei, 1564–1642

Nineteenth-Century Cocktail Creations: How to Mix Drinks: A Barkeeper's Handbook

Joanne Asala, Editor
Historic Cookbooks of the World

Rowan Grier, Series Editor
Classic Cocktail Guides
and Retro Bartender Books

Classic Cocktail Guides and Retro Bartender Books and *Historic Cookbooks of the World* are published by Kalevala Books, an imprint of Compass Rose Technologies, Inc., PO Box 409095, Chicago, IL 60640. Titles published by Kalevala Books are available at special quantity discounts to use as premiums and sales promotions or for academic use. For more information, please write to the Director of Special Sales, Compass Rose Technologies, Inc., PO Box 409095, Chicago, IL 60640 or contact us through our Web site, www.CompassRose.com.

Editors' Note

Some ingredients found in vintage cocktail guides are unavailable or hard to come by today. Check out our resource guide at the back for vendors who specialize in hard-to-find ingredients and websites with information on how to recreate classic cocktails and cocktail ingredients.

ISBN: 978-1-880954-30-0

Classic Cocktail Guides and Retro Bartender Books

Historic Cookbooks of the World

Orinoco Bitters.

Superior to any Angostura in the World.

Whenever tried it is admitted
to be the best article known
for bar use. Especially adapted
for bar use. Sample free on
application.

MAX D. STERN,

SOLE PROPRIETOR,

32 Water Street,

Near Broad, **NEW YORK.**

INDEX

Historic Cookbooks of the World

BAR ROOM GLASSWARE

—AND—

FIXTURES

A Larger Assortment

**AND AT LOWER
- PRICES THAN -
- ANYWHERE- -
—— ELSE. ——**

An almost endless variety of all goods required in

RESTAURANTS,——

——HOTELS AND——

——BAR ROOMS.

EDWARD RORKE & CO.,

40 BARCLAY ST.,

NEW YORK.

Beadleston·&·Woerz,

Ales, Porter,
and Lager Beer,

Empire Brewery,

291 West 10th Street, New York.

Historic Cookbooks of the World

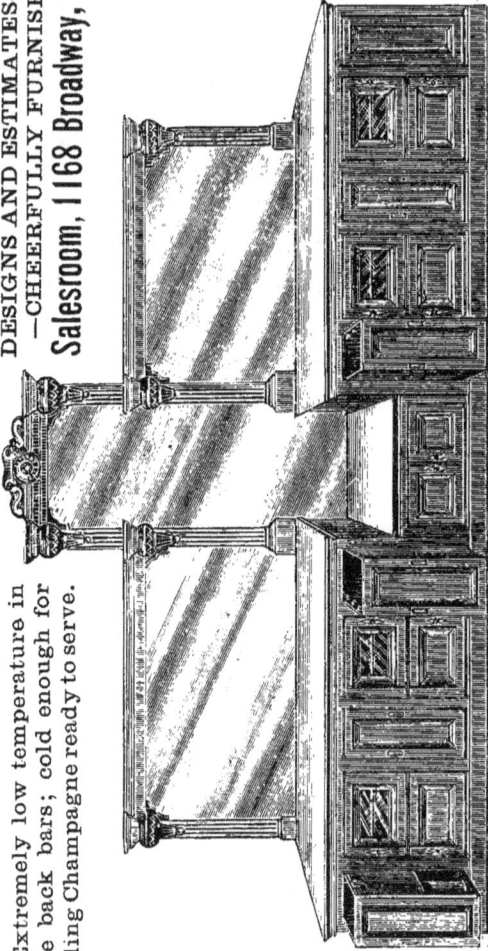

"LORILLARD" BACK BAR REFRIGERATOR.

DESIGNS AND ESTIMATES—
—CHEERFULLY FURNISHED.

Salesroom, 1168 Broadway, N. Y.

Extremely low temperature in these back bars; cold enough for chilling Champagne ready to serve.

THE DUTIES OF A BARTENDER.

Probably in no other branch of business is the person in charge brought so constantly in contact with people of every class and disposition, as is the bartender, and he should therefore be an intelligent man and a good judge of human nature. He should be at all times polite and attentive to customers, and present a neat and cheerful appearance, having a pleasant look and word for each one who favors him with his custom.

It is the great aim of a successful bartender to make as many friends and to control as much trade as possible, and the surest way of doing this is to pay the closest attention to the wants of patrons and making such an impression upon the mind of the customer, through furnishing a good article of the liquor called for, as well as serving in such a gentlemanly and artistic manner, as that he will remember the place, call again himself and recommend it to his friends. A bartender, like an actor, should never show that he is feeling unwell or in a bad humor, as it is calculated to make a bad impression on the patrons, who are to him what the public is to the actor. In short, he should sympathize with those who are not feeling well, appear jolly to those who are apparently light-hearted, and in general use good judgment in his conversation with all with whom he comes in contact while in the discharge of his duties.

With these few words on the general attributes of a good bartender, we will enter upon the details of his business.

Glasses of all the various kinds should be arranged on the bench so that they will be handy when wanted. When a man steps up to the bar the bartender should at once present himself before him, and, producing a glass of ice water upon the counter, ask the customer in a polite and pleasant tone of voice what kind of liquor he wishes.

All mixed drinks should be made in full view of the purchaser, and such skill and dexterity should be used in handling the bottles, glasses, etc., as will gain the admiration of the customer and establish the bartender as an expert in his profession.

Under no circumstances should a stained or dripping glass be handed out to a customer or used in mixing a drink, and it is always advisable to have a number of glasses about two-thirds filled with water and ice on the bench ready for use at any time, but the customer should not be expected to pour out the water from a pitcher as is sometimes done.

STOCK REQUIRED IN SALOON.

LIQUORS.

Brandy of several grades, Rye, Bourbon, Irish and Scotch Whiskey, Holland and Old Tom Gin, St. Croix and Jamaica Rum, Apple Jack, Blackberry, Alcohol and Arrac.

WINES.

Champagne, Claret, Rhine and Moselle, Madeira, Sauterne, Sherry, Burgundy, Port (red and white), Bordeaux-California, Catawba, Tokay, Spanish, Hungarian Wines (red and white).

ALES, PORTER AND BEER.

Scotch, Stock, New and Old Ales, Porter, Lager Beer.

BITTERS.

Orinoco, Peruvian, Angostura, Hostetter's, Stoughton, Boonecamp, Sherry Wine Bitters and Boker's Bitters.

MINERAL WATERS.

Ginger Ale (Belfast and Domestic), Kissingen, Apollinaris, Vichy, Seltzer and Soda Waters, Sarsaparilla and Cider.

SYRUPS, MIXTURES, ETC.

White Gum, Raspberry, Pineapple, Strawberry, Orange and Rock Candy Syrups, Honey, Tansy, Black Molasses, Jamaica Ginger, Peppermint, Red and Black Pepper, Eggs, Milk, Sugar (lumps and pulverized), Mint, Nutmeg, Cloves, Coffee, Cinnamon.

CORDIALS.

Chartreuse, Absinthe, Benedictine, Kimmel, Berlin Gilka, Curacoa (red and white), Anisette, Maraschino, Vermouth, Kirschwasser, Vanilla, Mint Cordial and Creme de Noyau.

BAR UTENSILS.

Measures of various sizes, from a gill to a gallon, Siphon, Ale and Beer Faucets, Funnels, Corkscrews, Hot-water Tank, Pitchers, Lemon Squeezers, Vents for Beer or Ale, Ice Cooler, Ice Pick, Ice Scoop, Ice Shaver, Gigger, Shaker, Long and Short-shanked Spoons, Strainers, Castor containing Spices, Ale Mugs, Cork-Pullers (several sizes), Champagne Faucets, Jugs, Syrup Pitchers, Lemon Knives, Scrubbing Brush, Corks of all sizes, Sugar Spoons, Tongs and Boxes, Egg-Breakers, Nutmeg and Graters, Bowls for Tom and Jerry, Sugar Punches, Pepper-Boxes, Fruit Dishes or Stands, Ladles, Brushes for scouring silver ware, Fruit Forks, Tray or Basket for Cigars, Labels, Comb and Brush, Matches, Wrapping and Writing Paper, Envelopes, Postal Cards and Stamps, City Directory, Ink, Mucilage, Newspapers, etc.. Demijohns, Bottles and Flasks, Straws, Sponge, Towels, Window, Scrubbing and Dusting Brushes.

The glassware necessary includes the following: Champagne, Claret, Port, Sherry and Rhine Wine Glasses, Cocktail Glasses for Champagne and also for Whiskey, etc., Julep and Cobbler Glasses, Absinthe, Whiskey, Pony Brandy, Hot Water, John Collins and Mineral-Water Glasses, as well as large Bar Glasses for mixing purposs and for ornamentation, together with all sizes of Beer, Ale and Porter Glasses.

There should also be a great variety of Fancy Glassware, to be used in decorating the shelves behind the counter, and there should also be such pieces of bric-a-brac, statuettes, pictures, etc., as will give the bar-room an attracttive appearance.

Fruits should be kept on hand with which to trim and flavor drinks as well as to attract the eyes of those who come to the place.

It is hardly worth while to mention in detail every article that would be found useful to the bar-tender, and we will therefore pass now to the main object of this book and give the recipes for preparing the various mixed drinks now in vogue.

———◆●◆———

LIST OF DRINKS.

————

MORNING GLORY FIZZ.

(Use large bar glass.)

Half tablespoonful of sugar;
Four to five dashes of lemon juice;
Three to four dashes of absinthe;
Dissolved well with little water;
One white of egg;
One wine glass of Scotch whiskey;
Fill the glass with fine shaved ice; shake well; strain in fancy bar glass; fill with plain soda or syphon seltzer.

————

EGG NOGG.

(Use large bar glass.)

One fresh egg;
Half tablespoon sugar;
Fill glass with shaved ice;
One pony glass St. Croix rum;

One wine glass of brandy;
Fill glass up with milk; shake well together; strain in
large bar glass; grate nutmeg on top and serve.

CHAMPAGNE SOUR.

(Use a fancy sour glass.)

One lump of loaf sugar, saturated with two dashes of
lemon juice; place in glass;
Fill up glass slowly with wine; stir well with spoon; ornament with fruit in season.

MILK PUNCH.

(Use large bar glass.)

Half tablespoon sugar;
Wine glass brandy;
Half wine glass St. Croix rum;
Fill glass with fine shaved ice; fill with fresh milk; shake
well together; strain in fancy bar glass; grate nutmeg on
top, then smile.

CURACOA PUNCH.

(Use large bar glass.)

Half tablespoon sugar; juice of quarter lemon; dissolve
well in a little water;
One wine glass of brandy;
One pony glass of Curacoa, red.
One-half pony glass of Jamaica rum;
Fill glass with shaved ice;
Shake well; ornament with fruit in season, and serve
with straws.

Gorham Plated Ware

FOR

RESTAURANT,
BAR AND HOTEL SERVICE.

Historic Cookbooks of the World

Gorham Plated Ware

FOR

RESTAURANT,
BAR AND HOTEL SERVICE.

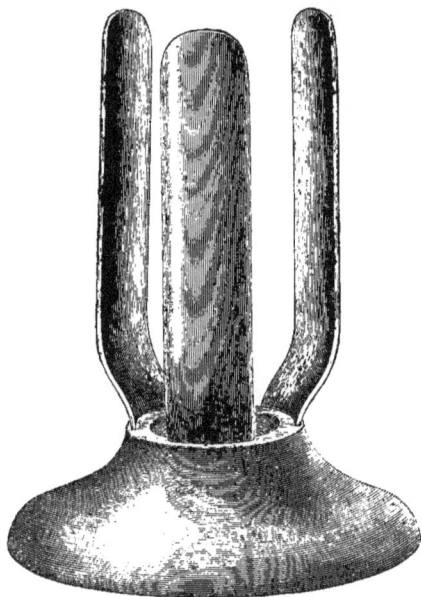

For Sale by the Jewelry Trade everywhere

GORHAM M'F'G CO.,

Silversmiths,

BROADWAY and 19th STREET,

NEW YORK.

Gorham Plated Ware

FOR

RESTAURANT,
BAR AND HOTEL SERVICE.

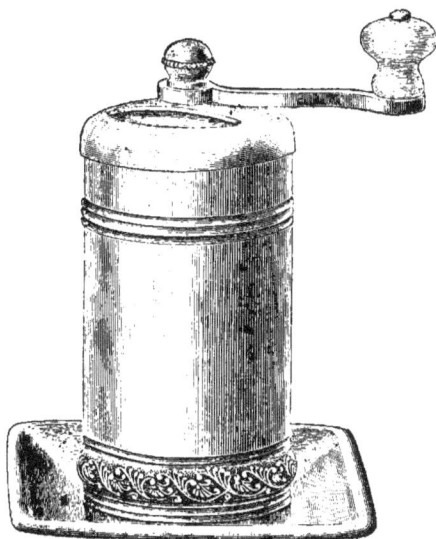

For Sale by the Jewelry Trade everywhere

GORHAM M'F'G CO.,

Silversmiths,

BROADWAY and 19th STREET,

NEW YORK.

BRANDY PUNCH.

(Use large bar glass.)

Half tablespoon of sugar;
Three to four raspberry syrup;
Juice of quarter lemon;
Use spoon and dissolve well in a little water;
Fill glass with shaved ice; add one and one-half wine glass Otard brandy; shake well; flavor with a few drops of Port wine; ornament with fruit in season and serve with straws.

PORT WINE PUNCH.

(Use large bar glass.)

Half tablespoon sugar;
Half tablespoon pineapple syrup;
Two or three dashes of lemon juice;
Dissolved with a little water;
Fill up with shaved ice; shake well; ornament with fruit in season and serve with straw.

GENERAL HARRISON EGG NOGG.

(Use large bar glass.)

One egg;
Three-quarters tablespoon sugar;
Fill glass with shaved ice; fill with cider; stir well with a spoon; strain in large bar glass; grate nutmeg on top and serve.

ST. CROIX RUM PUNCH.

(Use large bar glass.)

Small tablespoon of sugar;
Squeeze juice of half lemon;
Dissolve well in little water; one-half pony glass of Jamaica rum; add one wine glass of St. Croix rum; fill up with fine ice; dress with fruit; serve with straws.

MEDFORD RUM SOUR.

(Use large bar glass.)

Half tablespoon of sugar;
Four to five dashes of lemon juice;
One squirt of syphon Vichy;
Dissolve well;
One wine glass of Medford rum;
Fill the glass with shaved ice; stir with spoon; strain in fancy sour glass, and serve with fruit in season.

CHAMPAGNE COBBLER.

(Use large bar glass.)

Small tablespoon of sugar;
Dissolve well with a little water;
One and one-half wine glass of Champagne;
Fill the glass with fine ice; stir well; ornament with oranges, berries, pine apple, etc.; serve with straw.

ST. CHARLES PUNCH.

(Use large bar glass.)

Small tablespoonful of sugar;
Dissolve well with water;
One wine glass Port wine;
Add one pony glass brandy;
Shake well; dress top with pineapple, oranges, berries, etc., serve with straws.

BRANDY SANGAREE.

(Use large bar glass.)

One glass of brandy;
Half tablespoon of sugar;

Add small wine glass of water;

Two small lumps of ice;

Stir well and serve with a little nutmeg on top if desired, strain.

MINT JULEP.

(Use large bar glass.)

Small tablespoonful of sugar;

Four to five sprigs of mint;

Dissolve well with sugar and water until the flavor of the mint is well extracted; then take out the mint;

Add one and one-half wine glass of brandy;

Fill the glass with fine ice and shake well, then take three or four sprigs of mint, insert them in the centre of the ice to form the shape of a bouquet, and ornament with fruits in season; flavor with Port wine or Jamaica rum; serve with straw, then smile.

FANCY WHISKEY SMASH.

(Use large bar glass.)

Half tablespoonful of sugar;

Three to four sprigs of mint;

Dissolve well in a little water;

One wine glass of whiskey;

Fill glass with fine ice; stir well and strain in a sour glass, with fruits in season, and serve.

OLD STYLE WHISKEY SMASH.

(Use large bar glass.)

Small tablespoonful of sugar;

Three to four sprigs of mint;

Dissolve well with the sugar and water;

Fill the glass with shaved ice;

One wine glass of whiskey;

Mix well and serve in small whiskey glass, with fruit in season.

OLD WHISKEY SLING.

(Use small bar glass.)

One teaspoonful of sugar;

Dissolve in one-half glass of water;

Two small lumps of ice;

One wine glass of whiskey;

Mix well; grate a little nutmeg on top and serve.

GIN COCKTAIL.

(Use a large bar glass.)

Two to three dashes of gum syrup;

One to two dashes of Orinoco Bitters;

Two dashes of absinthe;

One wine glass Holland gin;

Fill with fine ice; stir well; squeeze from a lemon peel on top, and serve.

ABSINTHE COCKTAIL.

(Use large bar glass.)

Fill glass with ice;

Three to four dashes of gum syrup;

One to two dashes of Orinoco Bitters;

One to two dashes of Curacoa;

One-quarter wine glass of water;

Three-quarter wine glass of absinthe;

Stir it well with a spoon; strain in fancy cocktail glass; squeeze lemon peel on top, then serve.

MISSISSIPPI PUNCH.

(Use large bar glass.

Small tablespoonful of sugar;

T. C. LYMAN. H. L. GREENMAN.

T. C. LYMAN & CO.

BREWERS OF

PALE, BURTON and EAST INDIA

ALES

AND PORTER,

Emerald Brewery.

420 to 428 West 38th Street,

Bet. 9th and 10th Aves.,

NEW YORK.

Historic Cookbooks of the World

BUDWEISER BREWING CO.

(LIMITED.)

LAGER BEER

———

DEAN STREET,

Franklin Ave. & Bergen St.

BROOKLYN,

N. Y.

———

W. A. A. BROWN,

GENERAL MANAGER.

Dissolve well with half wine glass of water;

Three dashes lemon juice;

One-half wine glass of Jamaica rum;

One-half wine glass of Bourbon whiskey;

One wine glass of brandy;

Fill the glass with fine shaved ice; shake well; ornament with orange and fruit in season, then serve with straw.

GIN FIZZ.

(Use bar tumbler.)

One-half tablespoonful of sugar;

Three to four dashes of lemon juice;

Fill the glass half full of shaved ice;

One wine glass of Old Tom gin;

Mix well with a spoon, strain in a large bar glass, and fill with syphon seltzer, then smile.

BRANDY FIZZ.

(Use a bar tumbler.)

Half tablespoonful of sugar;

Four or five dashes of lemon juice;

One wine glass of brandy;

Fill the glass with shaved ice, stir well with a spoon, strain in fancy sour glass, fill up with syphon seltzer or Vichy and serve.

WHISKEY JULEP.

(Use a bar tumbler.)

One small tablespoonful of sugar;

Three to four sprigs of mint, dissolved well with a little water until the essence of mint is extracted;

One wine glass of whiskey;

Fill the glass with ice, stir well, ornament with fruits in season, flavor with Jamaica rum and serve.

SHERRY WINE PUNCH.

(Use large bar glass.)

One-half wine glass of pineapple syrup;
Two or three dashes of lemon juice;
Fill the glass with fine shaved ice;
One and one-half glass Sherry wine;
Mix well with spoon, ornament with fruits, and dash it off with a little claret wine, and serve with straws

APPLE JACK SOUR.

(Use large bar glass.)

One-half tablespoon of sugar;
Three or four dashes of lemon juice, dissolved well with a squirt of seltzer;
One wine glass of apple brandy;
Fill glass with fine ice;
Mix well, strain into a sour glass, ornament with fruit and serve.

SELTZER LEMONADE.

(Use large bar glass.)

One tablespoonful of sugar;
Four or five dashes of lemon juice;
Fill glass one-third full of fine ice;
Then fill with syphon seltzer, stir well with spoon while filling the glass with seltzer, then serve.

SODA COCKTAIL.

(Use a bar goblet.)

Four to five dashes of Orinoco Bitters;
Four to five lumps of fine ice;
Place one piece of lemon peel in glass;

One teaspoonful of sugar;
Fill up the glass with a bottle of lemon soda, stir well
with a spoon, then serve.

POUSSE CAFE.
(Use Sherry wine glass.)

Also use Sherry wine glass for mixing instead of a spoon,
it has a better appearance.

In mixing the above drink, each liquor should be sepa-
rated from each other.

One-sixth glass of raspberry syrup;
One sixth glass of Maraschino;
One-sixth glass of Curacoa, red;
One-sixth glass of Chartreuse;
One-sixth glass of kimmel;
One-sixth glass of brandy;
The above ingredients will fill your glass, then serve.

RHINE WINE COBBLER.
(Use large bar glass.)

One tablespoonful of sugar, dissolved in a little water;
One and a half wine glass of Rhine wine;
Fill the glass with ice;
Stir well with a spoon, and dress with fruit, and serve.

JERSEY COCKTAIL.
(Use large bar glass.)

One small tablespoonful of sugar;
Three to four dashes of Orinoco Bitters;
One wine glass full of cider;
Fill rest of glass with;
Mix well, twist a piece of lemon peel on top, and serve.

SILVER FIZZ.

(Use a bar goblet.)

One-half tablespoon of sugar.

Three or four dashes of lemon juice;

One egg, the white only;

One wine glass of Old Tom gin;

Fill the glass with fine shaved ice;

Shake well, strain in fizz glass, fill with syphon seltzer, and serve.

SHERRY WINE COBBLER.

(Use large bar glass.)

One small tablespoon of sugar, dissolved well with a little water;

Fill up the glass with shaved ice;

One and a half glass of Sherry wine;

Shake well, dress with fruit in season, and dash with Port wine, and serve with straws.

HOW TO MIX TOM AND JERRY.

(Use punch bowl for the mixture.)

Five pounds sugar;

Twelve eggs;

Half wine glass Jamaica rum;

One and a half teaspoonful of ground cinnamon;

Half teaspoonful of ground cloves;

Half teaspoonful of ground allspice;

Beat the white of the eggs to a stiff froth, and the yolks until they are as thin as water; then mix together and add the spice and rum, thicken with sugar until the mixture attains consistence of a light batter.

Classic Cocktail Guides and Retro Bartender Books

TO DEAL OUT TOM AND JERRY TO CUSTOMERS.

Take a small bar glass, and to one tablespoonful of the above mixture add one wine glass of brandy, fill the glass with boiling water and grate a little nutmeg on top, then serve.

Adepts at the bar, in serving Tom and Jerry, sometimes adopt a mixture of one-half brandy, one-fourth Jamaica rum, and one-half St. Croix rum, instead of brandy plain. This compound is usually mixed and kept in a bottle, and a wine glass is used to each tumbler of Tom and Jerry.

TOM AND JERRY COLD.

This drink is prepared the same as the hot Tom and Jerry, with the exception of using cold water.

JOHN COLLINS.

(Use extra large bar glass.)

Five or six dashes of lemon juice;
One small tablespoonful of sugar;
One wine glass full of Holland gin;
Fill one-third of fine ice;
Fill up with a bottle of plain soda, stir well with a spoon while filling with soda, remove the ice, then serve.

WHISKEY TODDY.

(Use a whiskey glass.)

One-half teaspoonful of sugar, dissolved in a little water;
One small lump of ice;
Place the glass with whiskey bottle on the bar before the customer to help himself.

HOT SCOTCH WHISKEY SLING.

(Use hot water glass.)

One piece of lump sugar;

Three-quarters full of hot water;

One piece of lemon peel;

One wine glass of Scotch whiskey;

Stir well with a spoon, grate a little nutmeg on top, then serve.

LEMONADE.

(Use large bar glass.)

One tablespoonful of sugar;

A little allspice dissolved with a little water;

One wine glass of Jamaica rum;

Fill the balance of glass with hot water, and grate a little nutmeg on top, and serve; if required, place a small portion of butter on top.

BRANDY SLING.

(Use hot water glass.)

One and one-half of lump sugar, dissolved in a little water;

One wine glass of brandy;

Fill balance with hot water;

Mix well with a spoon, and grate a little nutmeg on top, and serve.

HOT APPLE TODDY.

(Use hot apple toddy glass.)

One-half tablespoonful of sugar, dissolved well in a little hot water;

One small sized well roasted apple;

One wine glass of Apple Jack;

Fill up the rest of glass with hot water, and mix well with

a spoon, grate a little nutmeg on top, and serve with a small bar spoon.

MEDFORD RUM SMASH.
(Use large bar glass.)

One-half tablespoon of sugar, dissolved in half wine glass of water;

Three to four sprigs of mint. Press the mint well in the sugar so that the essence of the mint is extracted;

One wine glass of Medford rum;

Fill glass with fine shaved ice;

Mix well, strain in fancy sour glass, with fruit, and serve.

HOT GIN SLING.
(Use hot water glass.)

One lump of loaf sugar, dissolved in a little hot water;

One wine glass of Holland gin;

Fill up the glass with hot water;

Mix well with a spoon, grate a little nutmeg on top, and serve.

BRANDY SOUR.
(Use large bar glass.)

Four to five dashes of lemon juice;

One-half tablespoon of sugar;

One squirt of syphon seltzer, dissolve well with a spoon;

One wine glass of brandy;

Fill glass with fine ice;

Mix well, strain in fancy sour glass, ornament with fruit, and serve.

PORT WINE FLIP.
(Use large bar glass.)

One-half tablespoon of sugar;

One fresh egg;

Fill glass half full of fine ice;

One wine glass of Port wine;

Shake well, strain in flip glass, grate nutmeg on top, then smile.

STONE WALL.

(Use large bar glass.)

One teaspoon of sugar;

Two small lumps of ice;

One wine glass of whiskey;

One bottle of plain soda water;

Mix well with a spoon, remove the ice, and serve.

TOM COLLINS.

(Use extra size large bar glass.)

One small tablespoon of sugar;

Four to five dashes of lemon juice;

Fill glass one-quarter full of ice;

One wine glass of Old Tom gin;

One bottle of plain soda;

Stir up well with a spoon, remove ice, then serve.

ROMAN PUNCH.

(Use large bar glass.)

One half tablespoonful of sugar ;

One-half pony glass of raspberry syrup;

Three dashes of lemon juice dissolved with a little water;

Fill glass up with fine shaved ice;

One-quarter glass of Curacoa;

One-half wine glass of brandy;

One-half pony glass of Jamaica rum;

Shake well, ornament with fruits and serve.

GIN SMASH.

(Use large bar glass.)

One-half tablespoonful of sugar;

Three or four sprigs of mint, dissolved with a little water
until essence of the mint is extracted;

Fill three-quarters of fine ice;

One wine glass of Holland gin;

Mix well, strain in fancy sour, dress with fruit and serve.

MEDFORD RUM PUNCH.

(Use large bar glass.)

One small tablespoonful of sugar;

Three or four dashes of lemon juice well dissolved in a
little water;

Fill glass with fine ice;

One and one-half wine glass of Medford rum;

Mix well, dress with fruit in season and flavor with Jamaica
rum, then serve with straws.

HOT RUM.

(Use hot water glass.)

Two lumps of loaf sugar dissolved with a little hot
water;

One wine glass of Jamaica rum;

Fill balance with hot water;

Mix well with a spoon, grate a little nutmeg, then serve.

STONE FENCE.

(Use whiskey glass.)

One wine glass of whiskey;

Two small lumps of ice;

Fill balance of glass with cider;
Mix well with a spoon, then serve.

PORT WINE PUNCH.

(Use bar goblet.) ·

One–half tablespoonful of sugar;
Two or three dashes of lemon juice, the juice of an or-
ange squeezed into it;
Dissolve with a little water;
Fill glass with fine ice;
One-half wine glass of Port wine;
Mix well, ornament with fruit, then serve with straws.

GIN TODDY.

(Use whiskey glass.)

One-half teaspoonful of sugar dissolved well in a little
water;
One lump of broken ice;
Place spoon in glass, then hand out the bottle of gin to
customer to help himself.

HOT IRISH PUNCH.

(Use hot water glass.)

Two lumps of loaf sugar;
One squirt of lemon juice;
Dissolve in a little hot water;
One wine glass of Irish whiskey;
Fill balance with hot water;
Mix well with spoon, put a little slice of lemon into it,
grate nutmeg on top and serve.

A. LIEBLER & CO.

D. G. YUENGLING, JR.'S

EXTRA FINE

Lager Beer,

128th St. & 10th Ave.

New York.

——— •◦•◦• ———

Telephone Call, 33 Harlem, or by Mail will receive prompt attention.

GEO. RINGLER & CO'S.
LAGER BIER
BREWERY E.92nd ST. BET. 2nd. 3rd AVE
NEW YORK.

Classic Cocktail Guides and Retro Bartender Books

SODA LEMONADE

(Use bar goblet.)

Four to five dashes of lemon juice ;

One tablespoonful of sugar ;

Fill glass half full of fine ice ;

One bottle of plain soda water;

Mix well with spoon, remove ice, and serve.

GIN JULEP.

(Use large bar glass.)

One small tablespoonful of sugar ;

Four to five sprigs of mint dissolved in one-half wine
glass of water until the essence of mint is extracted;

Fill the glass with fine ice ;

One and one-half glass of Holland gin;

Mix well with a spoon; ornament in same way as Mint
Julep, then smile.

PORTER SANGAREE.

(Use large bar glass.)

One-half tablespoon of sugar dissolved well in one wine
glass of water ;

Four to five lumps of fine broken ice ;

Fill rest of glass with porter;

Stir well with spoon, remove the ice, and grate nutmeg
on top, and serve.

BRANDY FIX.

(Use large bar glass.)

One-half tablespoon of sugar ;

Tree dashes of lemon juice ;

Four to five dashes of pineapple syrup ;

Dissolve well with a little water ;
Fill glass with fine ice ;
One wine glass of brandy ;
Mix well, dress with fruits, and serve with straws.

BRANDY FLIP.
(Use a large bar glass.)
One small tablespoonful of sugar ;
One fresh egg ;
One-half glass of fine ice ;
One wine glass of brandy;
Shake well, strain in a fancy bar glass. grate a little nutmeg on top, and serve.

WHISKEY SOUR.
(Use large bar glass.)
Half tablespoonful of sugar ;
Four to five dashes of lemon juice ;
One squirt of syphon Vichy ;
Dissolve well ;
Fill glass with ice ;
One wine glass of whiskey ;
Stir well, strain in sour glass, dress with fruit, and smile.

ST. CROIX FIX.
(Use large bar glass.)
Three to four dashes of lemon juice ;
One-half tablespoon of sugar ;
One-half pony of pineapple syrup ;
Dissolve well in a little water with a spoon ;
Fill glass with shaved ice ;
One wine glass of St. Croix rum;
Mix well, ornament with fruit, and serve with straw.

SHERRY WINE SANGAREE.

(Use whiskey glass.)

One teaspoon of sugar, dissolve well in a little water ;
Two lumps of broken ice ;
One wine glass of Sherry wine;
Mix well, grate nutmeg on top, remove the ice, and serve.

PORT WINE COBBLER.

(Use large bar glass.)

One-half tablespoon of sugar;
One pony glass of raspberry syrup;
One and one-half wine glass of Port wine;
Fill with fine shaved ice, mix well, and serve with fruit in season.

GIN SOUR.

(Use bar tumbler.)

One-half tablespoon of sugar;
Three to four dashes of lemon juice;
One squirt of syphon seltzer; dissolve well;
One wine glass of Holland gin;
Fill with fine shaved ice, mix well, strain in fancy sour glass, ornament with fruits, and serve.

GIN FIX.

(Use large bar glass.)

One-half tablespoon of sugar;
Three to four dashes lemon juice;
One half pony glass raspberry syrup, dissolved well in a little water;
One wine glass of Holland gin;
Fill glass up with fine shaved ice, mix well with spoon, dress top with fruits, then serve with straw.

COLD BRANDY PUNCH.

(Use whiskey glass.)

One-half teaspoon of sugar;

Dissolve the sugar with a little water, place spoon in, then hand out the bottle and glass to customer to help himself.

WHISKEY SMASH.

(Use a large bar glass.)

One-half tablespoon of sugar;

Four to five sprigs of mint; dissolve well until the essence of the mint is extracted;

Fill glass half full of ice;

Wine glass of whiskey;

Mix well, strain into a sour glass, dress with fruit in season and serve.

ST. CROIX SOUR.

(Use a large bar glass.)

One-half tablespoon of sugar;

Three to four dashes of lemon juice;

One squirt of syphon Vichy, dissolved well with a spoon;

One wine glass full of shaved ice;

Fill up with water, mix well, strain in fancy sour glass, serve with fruits in season.

EGG LEMONADE.

(Use a large bar glass.)

Four to five dashes of lemon juice;

One tablespoon of sugar;

One fresh egg;

Fill glass three-quarters full of ice, fill the balance with water, shake well, then strain into a large fancy bar glass, and serve.

Fill the glass three-quarters full of fine ice;

One wine glass of whiskey;

Stir well with a spoon and strain in a fancy cocktail glass, and squeeze the oil from a lemon peel on top, then serve.

BRANDY AND SODA.

(Use a large bar glass.)

Three or four small lumps of ice;

One wine glass of brandy;

One bottle of plain soda;

Stir up well with a spoon and serve.

'ARF AND' ARF.

(Use a large ale glass.)

Fill glass half-full of porter and the balance with ale, then serve.

EGG MILK PUNCH.

(Use a large bar glass.)

One small tablespoon of sugar;

One fresh egg;

Fill glass half-full of fine ice;

One wine glass of brandy;

One pony glass of St. Croix rum;

Fill up with fresh milk, shake well together until it becomes a stiff cream, strain in a large glass, grate a little nutmeg on top and serve.

RHINE WINE AND SELTZER.

(Use a wine glass.)

Fill the glass three-quarters full of Rhine wine and balance of glass with syphon seltzer or Vichy, then serve.

AMERICAN STYLE OF MIXING ABSINTHE.
(Use a large glass.)

Fill your glass three-quarters full of fine ice;

One pony glass of absinthe;

One-half pony glass anisette;

Two wine glasses of water;

Shake well until the outside of the shaker is covered with ice; strain in a larger bar glass and serve.

FRENCH STYLE OF MIXING ABSINTHE.
(Use an absinthe glass.)

One pony glass of absinthe;

Take the top part of your absinthe glass, fill with fine shaved ice and the balance with water; then raise the absinthe bowl up high until the water has run through; then pour into a large bar glass and serve.

BRANDY AND GINGER ALE.
(Use a large bar glass.)

Two small lumps of broken ice;

One wine glass of brandy;

One bottle of ginger ale;

Mix well together, then serve. Particular attention must be paid when pouring the ginger ale into the other mixtures not to let the foam run over the glass, and it is customary to ask the customer what kind of ale he desires, the Stand - ard Ginger Ale in Codd's Globe stoppered bottles being the best in use, as it mixes better and will give more satisfaction than any other.

WHISKEY COBBLER.
(Use large bar glass.)

Onehalf tablespoon of sugar;

In Codd's Patent Bottles.

STANDARD Bottling Co. Ginger Ale.
EQUAL TO BEST IMPORTED.

STANDARD Bottling Co. Lemon Soda

STANDARD Bottling Co. Sarsaparilla.

STANDARD Bottling Co. Cider.

Our Carbonated Beverages

are enjoying a wide reputation, as in point of PURITY and
GENERAL EXCELLENCE they favorably compare with
the best manufactures of their class.

Our Ginger Ale

**Is a Specialty, and embodies all the characteristics of the imported, and
at a lower price.**

We bottle in the "*Codd Bottle*," which in addition to
being *cleaner* than a cork is *less trouble* to the
Bartender *in opening* and much more
rapidly handled.

STANDARD BOTTLING CO.,
630 Grand St,

JERSEY CITY.

—THE—
=CHECK REGISTER=
—AND—
CHECK RECEPTACLE
—FOR—
BARS, RESTAURANTS

THIS IS THE ONLY SAFEGUARD TO THE CASH RECEIPTS OF ANY BUSINESS.

CAN BE MADE TO FIT ANY SPACE—AND CONTAINS CHECKS SUFFICIENT TO RUN ANY BUSINESS.

AND LIQUOR SALOONS.

JOHN CASEY, INVENTOR AND PATENTEE.

Office and Factory:
575 GROVE STREET
—AND—
197 AND 199 THIRTEENTH STREET,
JERSEY CITY, N. J.

One-half pony glass of pineapple syrup;
Dissolve with a little water;
Fill up glass with fine ice;
One wine glass of whiskey;

Mix well and dress with fruits in season, then serve with straw.

WHISKEY AND CIDER.

(Use whiskey glass.)

Place your bottle of whiskey before the customer to help himself; then fill up the glass with cider, stir with spoon and serve.

TURF CLUB COCKTAIL.

Two or three dashes of Peruvian Bitters;
One-half wine glass of Tom gin;
One-half wine glass of Italian Vermouth;

Fill glass three-quarters full of fine ice, stir well with spoon and strain in fancy cocktail glass, then serve.

SAM WARD.

(Use fancy cocktail glass.)

Fill the same with fine crystal ice;
One-half wine glass of Chartreuse;
One-half wine glass of Curacoa;

Stir well with a spoon, peel the rind of a lemon the same as you would an apple, dip in sugar and place on top in tasty manner, then serve.

SHERRY AND EGG.

(Use a whiskey glass.)

Place a small portion of sherry in the glass to prevent the egg from sticking to the glass, then break a cold egg into it, hand this out to the customer, also the bottle of Sherry wine to help himself.

GOLDEN FIZZ.

(Use a large bar glass.)

Two to three dashes of lemon juice;

One small tablespoon of sugar;

One wine glass of Old Tom gin;

One egg, the yolk only;

Fill the glass three–quarters full of fine ice;

Shake well with shaker, strain in fancy fizz glass, fill the balance with syphon seltzer, and serve.

OLD TOM GIN COCKTAIL.

(Use a large bar glass.)

One to two dashes of Orinoco Bitters;

Two or three dashes of gum syrup;

One or two dashes of absinthe;

Fill the glass with fine shaved ice;

One wine glass of Old Tom gin;

Stir well with a spoon, strain in a fancy cocktail glass, twist the oil from a piece of lemon peel on top, then serve.

WHISKEY COCKTAIL.

((Use a large glass.)

One or two dashes of bitters;

Two or three dashes of gum syrup;

One or two dashes of absinthe;

Classic Cocktail Guides and Retro Bartender Books

FRED. NEUMER,

----BOTTLER OF----

Geo. Ehret's - - - New York.
" " Franciskaner " "
Jos. Schlitz Brewing Co's - Milwaukee.
Rochester, Cincinnati and Imported

For the Trade, Family Use and Export.

155 & 157 West 20th Street,

Bet. 6th & 7th Aves. New York.

HADDOCK & LANGDON.
BREWERS & MALTSTERS
408-414 East 14th Street,
NEW YORK.

A L E A N D P O R T E R F O R B O T T L I N G.

Pale XXX, XX and Amber Ale.

Burton, East India, XXX and XX Stock Ale, Porter and Brown Stout.

⇢✦HERMANN✦⇠

LAGER BEER BREWERY,

BURR, SON & CO., Proprietors.

221, 223, 225, 227, 232 & 234
WEST 18TH STREET,
NEW YORK.

FANCY BRANDY SMASH.

(Use a large bar glass.)

One half tablespoon of sugar, dissolved in a little water;

Three or four springs of mint, dissolved well;

One wine glass of brandy;

Fill with ice, stir up well with a spoon, strain in fancy glass and serve with fruit in season.

JAMAICA RUM SOUR.

(Use a large bar glass.)

One-half tablespoon of sugar;

Three or four dashes of lemon juice, dissolved well with a squirt of syphon seltzer;

One wine glass of Jamaica rum;

Fill glass three-quarters with water, mix well, strain in fancy sour glass, and serve with fruits.

SHERRY FLIP.

(Use a bar tumbler.)

One egg;

One-half tablespoon of sugar, fill glass half full of shaved ice;

One and one-half glass Sherry wine;

Shake well, strain in fancy bar glass, grate a little nutmeg on top, then serve.

WHISKEY FIZZ.

(Use large bar glass.)

One-half tablespoon of sugar;

Three or four dashes of lemon juice, dissolved well in a little water, fill the glass with fine ice;

One wine glass of whiskey;

Mix well with a spoon, strain in large glass, and fill with syphon seltzer and serve.

MANHATTAN COCKTAIL.

(Use large bar glass.)

Two or three dashes of Peruvian Bitters;
One to two dashes of gum syrup;
One-half wine glass of whiskey;
One-half wine glass of Vermouth;
Fill glass three-quarters full of fine shaved ice, mix well with a spoon, strain in fancy cocktail glass and serve.

GIN PUFF.

(Use large fancy bar glass.)

One wine glass of Holland gin;
Fill the glass half full of fresh milk and the balance with syphon seltzer, then serve.

Jacob & Josef Kohn,

VIENNA, AUSTRIA,

New York Depot, 814 Broadway,

Inventors and Manufacturers of the Celebrated

Vienna Bent Wood Furniture,

The Only Unbreakable Chair!

CALL AND SEE OUR CHAIRS AND TABLES
BEFORE BUYING ELSEWHERE.

OPPERMANN & MULLERS

TURTLE BAY

LAGER BEER

BREWERY

TRADE MARK

44TH & 45TH STS BETWEEN 1ST & 2ND AVES NY

Warneck & Toffler,

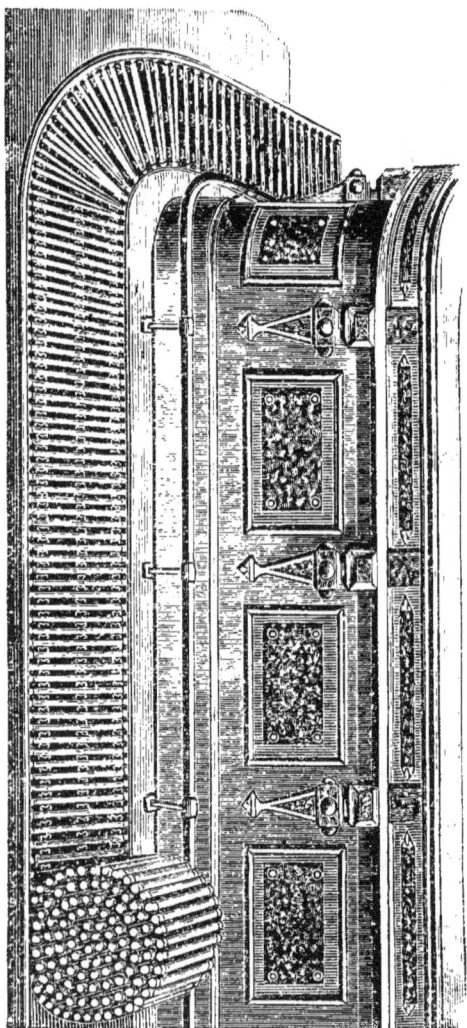

Well known Toffler Rolling Wood Matting.

MANUFACTURERS OF THE

2 1 1 E. 22d St. ($^{NEAR}_{3D\ AVE.}$) New York.

EXTRACTS

FROM THE

EXCISE LAW

OF THE

STATE OF NEW YORK.

SECTION VII.

Persons to whom licenses may be granted.

Amount to be paid therefor.

Application for licenses to be posted in room where sales are made.

Evidence.

Record to be kept.

Sales in quantities of five gallons and over.

SECTION 7. The board of excise in any city, town or village shall have the power to grant license to any person or persons of good moral character, who shall be approved by them, permitting him or them to sell and dispose of, at any one named place, within such city, town or village, strong or spirituous liquors, wines, ale or beer in quantities less than five gallons at a time upon receiving a license fee, to be fixed in their discretion, and which shall not be less than thirty dollars, nor more than $150, in any town or village; and not less than thirty dollars nor more than $250 in any city. Such licenses shall only be granted on written application to the said board, signed by the applicant or applicants, specifying the place for which license is asked, and the name or names of the applicant or applicants, and of every person interested or to be interested in the business to authorize which the license shall be used; and the license shall be kept posted, by the person or persons licensed, in a conspicuous position in the room or place where his or their sales are made, and shall be exhibited at all times by the person or persons so licensed, and by all persons acting under such license, on demand, to every sheriff, constable or officer, or member of police. Any omission so to display and exhibit such certificate shall be presumptive evidence that any person or persons so omitting to display and exhibit the same has and have no license. The said board of excise shall keep a complete record of the names of all persons licensed, as herein provided, with a statement of the place licensed, and license fee imposed and paid in each case, which record they shall at all times permit to be seen, in a convenient place at their principal office in any city, or at the clerk's office in any town or village. Persons not licensed may keep, and, in quantities not less than five gallons at a time, sell and dispose of strong and spirituous liquors, wines, ale and beer, provided that no part thereof shall be drank or used in the building, garden or inclosure communicating with, or in any public street or place contiguous to the building in which the same be so kept, disposed of or sold. (*Section* 4, *chap.* 175, 1870, *as amended by sec.* 2, *chap.* 549, 1873.)

The commissioners are liable, criminally, for an unlawful and corrupt exercise of the powers vested in them. While they are responsible only for good faith and integrity, they cannot from corrupt motives either grant or withhold a license improperly, and shield themselves under the judicial character of their office. (*The People* v. *Jones et al.*, 54 *Barb. Sup. Court R.*, 311.)

SMITH & RADLEY,

FORMERLY

SMITH & GREENOUGH,

MAKERS OF

FINE

CABINET BARS

225 & 227 East 36th St.,

NEW YORK.

OCHS & LEHNERT'S

AETNA

Lager Beer Brewery,

Cor. Bushwick Ave. & Scholes St.,

BROOKLYN, E. D.

THOMAS MILLER,

SHEET METAL BAR APPLIANCES

MANUFACTURER OF FIRST-CLASS

MILLER'S PATENT ALE AND BEER MEASURES.

—ALSO SOLE MANUFACTURER OF—

MILLER'S PATENT HEAT-SAVING HOT WATER URNS.

MILLER'S PATENT LIQUOR MIXER AND STRAINER.

MILLER'S PATENT LIQUOR MIXER AND STRAINER.

MILLER'S IMPROVED STOP FUNNELS.

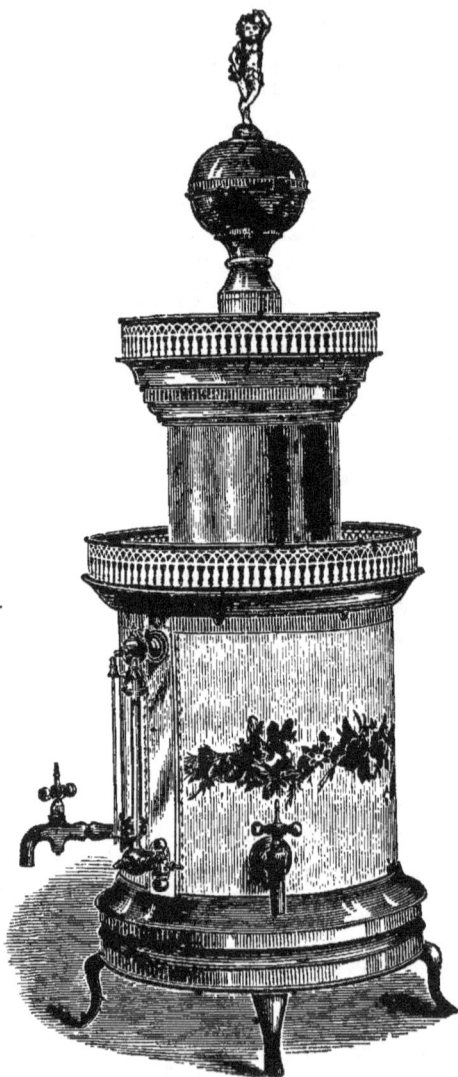

No. 118 Worth St. (—NEAR— ELM STREET.) New York.

Classic Cocktail Guides and Retro Bartender Books

Since the statute requires a license to be in writing, defendant cannot justify under a parol license.

CHAPTER 340.

An Act to regulate the sale of intoxicating liquors in cities having a population of over three hundred thousand inhabitants.

Passed April 30, 1883, three-fifths being present.

The People of the State of New York, represented in Senate and Assembly, do enact as follows:

SECTION 1. The Boards of Commissioners of Excise in the cities of this State having a population of over three hundred thousand inhabitants, shall, if all other requirements of the law have been complied with, have power to grant license to sell strong or spirituous liquors, ale, wine or beer, to be drank on the premises, to be named in the application for such license, to any person or persons having a good moral character, whether or not they keep or propose to keep an inn, tavern or hotel, provided that no such license shall be granted unless the said commission rs shall be satisfied, upon examination, that the applicant therefor is a person of good moral character, and that a license may properly be granted for such sale in the place proposed.

§ 2. Any such board shall have at all times discretionary power to permit any person or persons to whom a license may have been granted, in respect of any specified premises, to remove to any other place within jurisdiction of the same board, during the period covered by such license, and there to continue the conduct of business under such license in the same manner as if no removal had been made, provided always that such discretionary powers shall not be exercised until, and unless all the requirements of law to be observed upon the granting of an original license, shall upon said application for removal be complied with and fulfilled in every respect.

§ 3. No person or persons having a license under this act, nor any assistant, agent, employee or servant of any such person or persons so licensed, shall be arrested for any alleged violation of any provision of any excise law, by any peace officer or other person, unless a warrant therefor, based on affidavit, shall have first duly issued according to law, except and provided that in case of any violation of any provision of any excise law between the hour of 1 o'clock Sunday morning and the hour of 12 o'clock Sunday night, in presence of any officer or person authorized to make arrests for violation of law. Such officer or person may forthwith and without warrant make arrest of the person or persons so violating any provision of any excise law.

Any officer or person authorized to make arrests for violation of law may arrest without warrant any person who, in the presence of such officer, or other person, authorized to make arrest, may be engaged in the sale of any intoxicating liquor without a license.

§ 4. No city of this State having a population of more than three hundred thousand inhabitants shall hereafter be subject to or be embraced within any provision of the sixth section of the Act, chapter six hundred and twenty-eight, of the Laws of eighteen hundred and fifty-seven, entitled "An Act to suppress intemperance, and to regulate the sale of intoxicating liquors," passed April sixteenth, eighteen hundred and fifty-seven.

§ 5. Any person who shall without a license sell or give away any strong or spirituous liquors, ale, wine or beer, to be drank upon the premises, shall be guilty of a misde meanor. And nothing in this Act contained shall alter or affect the provisions of existing laws touching the sale or giving away of intoxicating liquors to be drank upon the premises, or the prohibtion thereof in the cases mentioned in said laws, and the penalties prescribed therefor, except as provided in section four of this Act. And such provisions of existing laws as are applicable to persons who might thereby be licensed to sell intoxicating liquors to be drank upon the premises shall be applicable to persons who may be licensed under this Act, except as such laws are modified by the terms of this Act.

§ 6. This Act shall take effect immediately.

SECTION XI.

After an innkeeper's license expires, he is not liable for selling without license, by reason of the commissioners' neglect to meet.

Mayor, &c., of New York, 4 E. D. Smith, 142.
Same case, 1 Abbots, Prac. R., 344.

SECTION XXI.

No recovery for liquor trusted.

SECTION 21. No inn, tavern or hotel keeper who shall trust any person, other than those who may be lodgers in his house, for any sort of strong or spirituous liquors or wine, shall be capable of recovering the same by any suit. All securities given for such debts shall be void; and the inn, tavern or hotel keeper taking such securities with intent to evade this provision shall forfeit double the sum intended to be secured thereby. (*Sec.* 10, *chap.* 628, 1857.)

SECTION XX.

To put up a sign.

SECTION 20. Every inn, tavern or hotel keeper licensed under the provisions of this Act shall, within thirty days after obtaining his license, put up a proper sign on or adjacent to the front of his house, with his name thereon, indicating that he keeps an inn, tavern or hotel; and he shall keep up such sign during the time that he keeps an inn, tavern or hotel. For every month's neglect to keep up such sign he shall forfeit ten dollars. (*Section* 9, *chap.* 628, 1857.)

The terms "inn, tavern or hotel" are used synonymously by the statute of 1857, to designate what is ordinarily and popularly known as an inn or tavern, or place for the entertainment of travelers, and where all their wants can be supplied. (*The People* v. *Jones et al.*, 54 *Barb. Sup. Court Rep.*, *p.* 311; *Krohn* v. *Sweeney*, 2 *Daly*, 200.)

———

SECTION XXXII.

Not to sell to drunken persons.

SECTION 32. Whoever shall sell or give away any strong or spirituous liquors or wines, or shall suffer any such liquors or wines to be sold or given away under his direction or authority, to any intoxicated person, shall forfeit not less than ten or more than twenty-five dollars for each offense. (*Sec.* 18, *chap.* 628, 1857.)

50 Ind. 22; 90 Ills. 59.

The offense of selling liquor to an intoxicated person created by the excise law of 1857 (sec. 18, chap. 628), was not indictable and punishable as a misdemeanor.

People v. Hislop, 77 N. Y., 331.
Foote v. People, 56 N. Y., 322.
People v. Stevens, 13 Wend., 341.
Lane v. Brown, 16 Wend., 561.
People *ex rel.*, Hislop v. Cowles, County Judge, etc., 16 Hun., 577.

He is subject only to a fine of not less than ten nor more than twenty-five dollars.—*Id.*

JOHN RINTOUL,

PARK HILL BREWERY
LAGER BEER.

Eighty-Seventh St. & Fourth Avenue,

NEW YORK.

C. A. MAROTZKI,
Manufacturer of and Dealer in

Store, Bar & Office Fixtures,

OF EVERY DESCRIPTION.

Office, 60 NEW BOWERY,
Near Chatham Square,

Warerooms, 59 & 61 NEW BOWERY, & 9 OLIVER ST.

NEW YORK.

Offices, Stores, &c., Fitted up and Renovated with Neatness.

ICE BOXES AND ICE HOUSES
Of all kinds on Hand and Made to Order at Shortest Notice.

SECTION LV.

No liquors allowed in any room or building used for polling or registry purposes.

In cities and incorporated villages, no building or part of a building shall be designated as a registry or polling place in which, or any part of which, spirituous or intoxicating liquors are sold.

Laws 1872, chap. 570, sec. 16.

No lager beer, ale, wine or spirituous liquors shall be allowed on election day in any room used for election purposes.

Laws 1880, chap. 56, sec. 17.

———

SECTION XXXIV.

Not to sell to habitual drunkards or paupers.

SECTION 34. It shall not be lawful, under the provisions of this Act, to sell intoxicating liquors to any person guilty of habitual drunkenness, nor to any person against whom the seller may have been notified by parent, guardian, husband or wife from selling intoxicating liquors; and every party so selling or retailing intoxicating liquors shall, on proof thereof, before any court of competent jurisdiction, be deprived of his license to sell, and shall not be allowed a renewal of said license, and, in addition, on conviction, shall be punished by a fine of not less than twenty dollars, nor more than fifty dollars for each and every violation of the provisions herein set forth. If any inn, tavern or hotel keeper, or any person or persons whatsoever, knowingly (outside of any poorhouse) shall sell or give to any pauper or inmate of any poorhouse or almshouse strong or spirituous liquors or wines, such person or persons so offending shall be fined twenty five dollars and be guilty of a misdemeanor, and on conviction shall be imprisoned not more than sixty days. (*Sec.* 20, *chap.* 628, 1857.)

25 Ohio St. R. 584 ; 50 Ind. 22.

On an indictment for selling liquor, if defendant puts in evidence a license granted in a specified town, it may be shown in answer that he was not a resident of the town in which he obtained the license. The commissioners do not acquire a jurisdiction over non-residents by their own act in asserting it. (*People* v. *Davis*, 36 *N. Y. Rep.*, 77; *Same Case*, 32 *How. Prac. Rep.*, 442.)

25 Ohio St. R. 381.

SECTION XXXV.

Days upon which sales of liquors prohibited.

SECTION 35. No inn, tavern or hotel-keeper, or other person, shall sell or give away intoxicating liquors or wines on Sunday or upon any day on which a general or special election or town meeting shall be held, and within one-quarter of a mile from the place where such general or special election or town meeting shall be held, in any of the villages, cities or towns of this State, to any person what. ever as a beverage. In case the election or town meetings shall not be general throughout the State, the provisions of this section in such case shall only apply to the city, county, village, or town in which such election or town meeting shall be held. Whoever shall offend against the provisions of this section shall be guilty of a misdemeanor, and shall be punished for each offense by a fine of not less than thirty dollars nor more than two hundred dollars, or by imprisonment not less than five days nor more than fifty days, or both such fine and imprisonment at the discretion of the court. (*Sec.* 21, *chap.* 628, 1857, *as amended by sec.* 5, *chap.* 549, 1873.)

THOMAS FARRELL,

MANUFACTURER OF

ICE HOUSES,

OF ALL KINDS.

322 and 324 West 41st Street.

JOHN SORG,

MANUFACTURER AND BOTTLER

OF ALL KINDS

Mineral Waters,

647 ELEVENTH STREET.

Bet. 47th & 48th Sts.   NEW YORK.

—THE—

BRUNSWICK-BALKE-COLLENDER CO.

SUCCESSORS TO THE J. M. BRUNSWICK & BALKE CO.
AND THE H. W. COLLENDER CO.

BILLIARD

⊰AND⊱

Pool Table

MANUFACTURERS.

——OFFICE AND MANUFACTORY:——

FOOT 8th STREET, EAST RIVER,

——WAREROOM:——

860 B'way, cor. 17th St. (Union Square,)

New York.

Lager Beer,

FRESHNESS AND PURITY

TO BE HAD EVERYWHERE.

Classic Cocktail Guides and Retro Bartender Books

Classic Cocktail Resource Guide

Some ingredients found in vintage cocktail guides are unavailable or hard to come by today. However, the creation of historically accurate cocktails is a growing hobby and with a bit of Internet research, you will find recipes for bitters and syrups online, as well as manufacturers that are developing new product lines for the classic cocktail enthusiast.

Vendors
A short selection of online vendors selling bitters, mixers, syrups, wine, liqueurs, and spirits. This list is by no means complete but is a good place to start your search.

BevMo!
www.bevmo.com

Binny's Beverage Depot
www.binnys.com

The Bitter Truth
www.the-bitter-truth.com

Cocktail Kingdom
www.cocktailkingdom.com

Fee Brothers
www.feebrothers.com

Hi-Time Wine Cellars
www.hitimewine.net

Internet Wines and Spirits
www.internetwines.com

The Jug Shop
www.thejugshop.com

Monin Gourmet Flavorings
www.moninstore.com

Trader Tiki's Hand-Crafted Exotic Syrups
www.tradertiki.com

The Whiskey Exchange
www.thewhiskyexchange.com

General Interest
These sites provide background information on individual ingredients, suggestions for substitutes, current commercial availability, and recipes.

The Chanticleer Society
A Worldwide Organization of Cocktail Enthusiasts
www.chanticleersociety.org

Drink Boy
Adventures in Cocktails
www.drinkboy.com

The Internet Cocktail Database Ingredients Search
www.cocktaildb.com/ingr_search

Museum of the American Cocktail
www.museumoftheamericancocktail.org

WebTender Wiki
www.wiki.webtender.com

Coming Soon from
Classic Cocktail Guides
and Retro Bartender Books

Cooling Cups
and Dainty Drinks

A Collection of 19th-Century Cocktails Perfect
for Civil War Reenactments
and Victorian Theme Parties

William Terrington

Illustrations from
"American Dancing Master and Ball-Room Prompter"
by Elias Howe

Jack's Manual of Recipes for Fancy Mixed Drinks and How to Serve Them

A Pre-Prohibition Cocktail Book

J. A. Grohusko

ISBN: 978-1-880954-28-7

The Twentieth-Century Guide for Mixing Fancy Drinks

A Pre-Prohibition Cocktail Book

James C. Maloney

ISBN: 978-1-880954-29-4

Now Available from Classic Cocktail Guides
and Retro Bartender Books

The Ideal Bartender

Cocktails and Mixed Drinks
from the Years of the First World War

Tom Bullock
Bartender of the Pendennis Club, Louisville, Kentucky
and of the St. Louis Country Club

Introduction by George H. Walker
Grandfather to President George Herbert Walker Bush
and Great-Grandfather to President George Walker Bush

ISBN: 978-1-880954-31-7

Daly's Bartenders' Encyclopedia

A Pre-Prohibition Cocktail Book

Tim Daly

ISBN: 978-1-880954-32-4

The Complete Bartender

The Art of Mixing Cocktails, Punches,
Egg Noggs, Smashes, Sangarees, Slings,
Cobblers, The Fizz, Juleps, Flips, Toddys,
Crustas, and All Plain and Fancy Drinks
in the Most Approved Style

Albert Barnes

ISBN: 978-1-880954-33-1

Now Available from
Historic Cookbooks of the World

Recipes of the Highlands and Islands of Scotland

A Classic Scottish Cookbook

Compiled by
An Comunn Gaidhealach

Originally published as
"The Feill Cookery Book"

ISBN: 978-1-880954-25-6

Now Available from
Historic Cookbooks of the World

Recipes of Sweden

A Classic Swedish Cookbook

Compiled by
Inga Norberg

ISBN: 978-1-880954-27-0